Maurice Kirsch

The Best Pasta and Noodle Dishes

Pasta

Cookery Editor Sonia Allison

Series Editor Wendy Hobson

foulsham

Pasta – Versatile and Delicious

Pasta dough is made of just three simple ingredients: flour, water and a little salt. Egg pasta or noodles are made by adding eggs to the dough. There is an endless variety of shapes and types of pasta, it can be long and thin, short and fat, take the form of a tube or a spiral and can be filled or layered. There are also different kinds of doughs, flavoured with herbs and spices for making all kinds of delicious dishes.

Contents

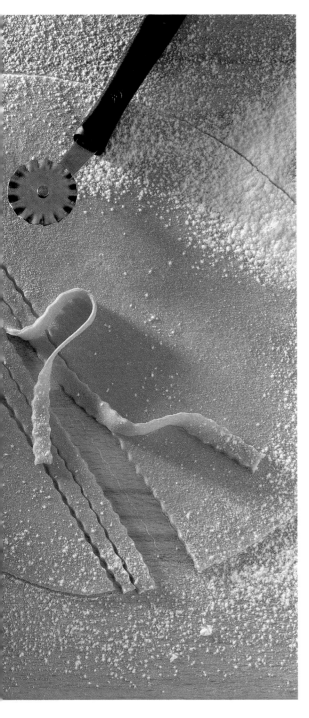

Brightly Coloured Pasta Shapes

Forms of pasta were
eaten and enjoyed in
ancient times by the
Etruscans, the Greeks,
the Romans and the
Chinese. Nowadays there
is a staggering variety of
pastas to choose from,
coming from all corners
of the world.

The History of Pasta Dough

People have been eating pasta for many centuries, but no one is sure about its exact origin. It is believed that the ancient Greeks and the Egyptians used a form of pasta in their cooking. Archaeologists have discovered wall paintings depicting Etruscan kitchen tools that resemble those used in the preparation of pasta, such as a pasta dough wheel. We also know that the Romans used long thin strips of pasta in their soups and used pasta in baked dishes. It was therefore probably no surprise to the people of Italy when Marco Polo brought noodles back from China. The Chinese had been making noodles since ancient times using not only wheat flour but also rice flour and flour made from beans.

We probably have the Arabs to thank for the long-keeping quality of pasta. They used to roll the dough out on to thin wooden sticks and leave it to dry in the sun. This nourishing form of food was invaluable to a nomadic people.

Spaghetti with sauce was a favourite dish at the German court of Ferdinand II and its popularity was the cause of an important invention. In those days, people ate pasta with their hands. However, the fashionable wide collars of the day got in the way, so members of the court started to use forks to eat their pasta; their long, thin three-pronged forks were not very good for the job, so someone introduced a new, smaller fork with four prongs, just like the ones we use today.

As pasta increased in popularity in Italian cooking, and from there spread to the rest of the world, an industry in dried pasta grew up. This originated from Arab-occupied Sicily. Later, Naples and Genoa became centres of dried pasta-making. Now varieties of pasta dishes are enjoyed the world over and interesting, new variations are always being created.

About the Recipes

1 Do not mix metric, Imperial or American measures. Follow one set only

2 Spoon measurement are level.

3 Eggs are size 3.

4 Kcals and kJs given ar approximate.

5 Preparation times include both preparatic and cooking times an are approximate.

6 Most recipes use whit pepper, but you can sut stitute black pepper if yo prefer. Pepper is alway best freshly ground.

7 Fresh lemon juice preferable for seasonin fish, but you can use bo tled lemon juice necessary.

8 Seasoning is very muc a matter of taste, so d taste as you cook and ad the level of seasoning yo prefer.

Quick Pasta Dishes

We are always short of time! Most people come home tired from work and the last thing they want to do is to spend a long time cooking the evening meal. A quick pasta dish is the obvious answer. It requires little work to prepare and can be enjoyed at your leisure.

Spaghetti with Beetroot, page 16

Spaghetti with Beetroot

Serves 4
Preparation time: 25 mins
2000 kcal/8400 kJ

---

225 g/8 oz spaghetti

1 or 2 sprigs fresh thyme

225 g/8 oz beetroot, cooked and peeled

1 shallot, finely chopped

25 g/1 oz/2 tbsp butter

salt and pepper

50 ml/2 fl oz/¼ cup dry white wine

150 ml/¼ pt/⅔ cup double cream

2 egg yolks

---

1 Cook the spaghetti in plenty of boiling salted water until al dente. Drain and rinse in hot water.
2 Meanwhile, wash the thyme and reserve some for decoration.
3 Halve the beetroots and cut half into slices and half into strips.
4 Fry the shallot gently with the thyme, beetroot strips and half the butter. Season to taste with salt and pepper and pour in the wine.
5 Fry the beetroot slices in the remaining butter and season to taste with salt and pepper. Arrange the beetroot slices and spaghetti on warmed plates.

6 Whip the cream until stiff, then stir in the egg yolks. Add this thickener to the beetroot strips and bring to the boil. Season to taste with salt, pepper or extra wine if necessary.
7 Pour the sauce with the beetroot strips over the spaghetti and decorate with the reserved thyme.

Photograph page 14

Gourmet Tip
It is always a good idea to warm the plates before serving. Plates can be warmed in the oven at about 100°C/200°F/gas mark ¼. If there is not enough room in the oven, warm them in hot water then dry them straight away.

Tagliatelle with Basil and Butter

Serves 4
Preparation time: 20 min
2800 kcal/1760 kJ

---

450 g/1 lb tagliatelle

2 bunches fresh basil

100 g/4 oz/½ cup butter

1 shallot, finely chopped

a few tablespoons of water

salt and pepper

---

1 Cook the tagliatelle plenty of boiling, salte water until al dente. Dra and rinse in hot water.
2 Reserve a few bas leaves for decoration, ar chop the rest finely.
3 Sauté the shallot in little butter with half th basil. Add the tagliatel to the pan and season taste with salt and peppe
4 Add the remaining bas with a little more butt and a few tablespoons water. Adjust the seaso ing if necessary.
5 Use a spoon to stir th remaining butter into th hot sauce. Take care th the sauce does not b any further. Arrange warmed plates and ga nish with basil leaves.

Photograph opposite

Spaghetti Gorgonzola

Serves 4
Preparation time: 25 mins
3000 kcal/12600 kJ

400 g/*14 oz* spaghetti
150 g/*5 oz* Gorgonzola
250 ml/*8 fl oz*/1 cup double cream
salt and pepper
25 g/*1 oz*/2 tbsp butter
2 egg yolks

1 Cook the spaghetti in plenty of boiling salted water until *al dente*.
2 Meanwhile, reserve a piece of cheese for decoration and remove the rind from the rest of the cheese. Melt the cheese slowly over a gentle heat with 100 ml/3^1/$_2$ fl oz/6^1/$_2$ tbsp double cream. Season sparingly with salt and pepper.
3 Drain the spaghetti and rinse in hot water. Season to taste with salt and pepper and swirl in the butter.
4 Whip the remaining cream until stiff, then stir in the egg yolks. Bring the sauce to the boil and stir in the cream and egg thickener. Reheat and adjust the seasoning if necessary.
5 Arrange the spaghetti on warmed plates, pour over the sauce and garnish with the reserved cheese.

Photograph (right)

Salami Spaghetti with Orange Sauce

Serves 4
Preparation time: 25 mins
2950 kcal/12390 kJ

*450 g/**1 lb** spaghetti*
juice from 4 oranges
salt
*50 g/**2 oz**/¹/₄ cup butter*
pepper
*100 g/**4 oz** salami, thinly sliced*

1 Cook the spaghetti in plenty of boiling salted water until *al dente*.
2 Meanwhile, boil the orange juice until it resembles a syrup. Salt it lightly but do not add pepper.
3 Drain the spaghetti and rinse in hot water. Swirl half the butter into the pan. Season to taste with salt and pepper and divide between warmed plates.
4 Bring the sauce to the boil, then turn off the heat. Stir in the rest of the butter, a piece at a time.
5 Arrange the salami slices on the plates with the spaghetti. Pour over the sauce and serve immediately.

Photograph (left)

Cheesey Rainbow Noodles

Serves 4
Preparation time: 20 mins
2300 kcal/9660 kJ

---

450 g/1 lb thin coloured egg noodles

250 ml/8 fl oz/1 cup double cream

100 g/4 oz Emmenthal cheese, grated

2 egg yolks

salt and pepper

25 g/1 oz/2 tbsp butter

a few chives, chopped

---

1 Cook the noodles in plenty of boiling salted water until *al dente*.
2 Meanwhile, bring 100 ml/3½ fl oz/6½ tbsp cream to the boil, then stir in three-quarters of the cheese.
3 Whip the remaining cream, then stir in the egg yolks. Add this thickener to the cheese sauce. Season to taste with salt and pepper and reheat, stirring constantly.
4 Drain the noodles and rinse in hot water. Melt the butter in a pan and swirl in the drained noodles with a few tablespoons of water.
5 Divide the sauce between warmed plates and place the noodles on top. Sprinkle with the rest of the cheese and the chives.

Photograph opposite (top)

Spinach Tagliatelle with Mushrooms

Serves 4
Preparation time: 25 mins
1400 kcal/5880 kJ

---

450 g/1 lb spinach tagliatelle

225 g/8 oz mushrooms, cut into eighths

1 shallot, finely chopped

3 cloves garlic, finely chopped

40 g/1½ oz/3 tbsp butter

25 g/1 oz parsley, finely chopped

30 ml/2 tbsp dry white wine or water

salt and pepper

a pinch of grated nutmeg

30 ml/2 tbsp water

---

1 Cook the tagliatelle in plenty of boiling salted water until *al dente*.
2 Cook the mushrooms, shallot and garlic in 15 g/½ oz/1 tbsp butter until the juices run from the mushrooms.
3 Add the parsley and the wine or water. Season to taste with salt, pepper and nutmeg.
4 Drain the tagliatelle and rinse in hot water. Return the tagliatelle to the pan, stirring in another 15 g/½ oz/1 tbsp butter and 30 ml/2 tbsp water. Season with salt and pepper and arrange on warmed plates.

5 Add the remaining bu ter to the mushroom m ture and serve the sau mixed with the tagliatel

Photograph opposite (bottom)

Gourmet Tip
If the central part of a garlic clove is green, it should be removed, otherwise the garlic flavour will be too strong.
When buying mushrooms, always look for the best quality heads with white, papery skins.

20

Rigatoni with Ham and Peppercorns

Serves 4
Preparation time: 30 mins
2250 kcal/9450 kJ

---

*450 g/**1 lb** rigatoni*

*100 g/**4 oz** uncooked gammon, cut into strips*

*25 g/**1 oz**/2 tbsp butter*

1 shallot, finely chopped

*250 ml/**8 fl oz**/1 cup double cream*

salt and pepper

*30 ml/**2 tbsp** red peppercorns*

*30 ml/**2 tbsp** green peppercorns*

2 egg yolks

---

1 Cook the rigatoni in plenty of boiling salted water until *al dente*.
2 Fry half the gammon very gently in half the butter. Add the shallot to the pan, pour in 100 ml/3¹/₂ fl oz/6¹/₂ tbsp cream and season lightly with salt and pepper. Fry the rest of the gammon in a separate pan with a quarter of the peppercorns.
3 Drain the rigatoni and rinse in hot water. Season to taste with salt and pepper. Return the rigatoni to the pan and swirl in the remaining butter.

4 Carefully bring the sauce to the boil, adding the remaining peppercorns. Whip the remaining cream, then stir in the egg yolks. Stir this thickener into the sauce. Bring back to the boil and season to taste with salt and a little pepper.
5 Divide the sauce between warmed plates. Add the rigatoni and place the fried gammon and peppercorns on top.
Variation
Back bacon can be used instead of gammon for this recipe.

Gourmet Tip
Rigatoni takes the form of a hollow pasta tube. It is recommended for dishes with sauce as the sauce clings well to the hollows.

Pasta and Noodle Dishes from Around the World

Tempting pasta and noodle dishes are served almost everywhere in the world. We do not know who first 'invented' pasta, but its popularity is certainly very widespread today. The following chapter gives you a taste of some of the dishes you may enjoy on your holidays – and can enjoy again in your own home.

Rice Noodles with Chicken and Mushrooms, page 26

25

Rice Noodles with Chicken and Mushrooms

Serves 4
Preparation time: 35 mins
1200 kcal/5040 kJ

---

25 g/*1 oz* dried Chinese mushrooms

350 g/*12 oz* rice noodles

350 g/*12 oz* chicken breast, skinned and cut into small pieces

25 g/*1 oz* root ginger, peeled and sliced

30 ml/*2 tbsp* soya or other cooking oil

1 shallot, finely sliced

1 small carrot, finely sliced

salt and pepper

4 shakes of soy sauce

1 bunch chives, coarsely chopped

---

1 Soak the mushrooms in lukewarm water. As soon as they are soft, drain and cut into thin strips.
2 Cook the noodles in plenty of boiling salted water until *al dente*.
3 Fry the chicken and ginger in the oil, then add the shallot and carrot.
4 Fry quickly over a high heat, mix in the mushrooms and pour in the soy sauce. Drain the noodles and add to the pan.
5 Season to taste with salt and pepper and flavour with more soy sauce, if liked. Mix in the chopped chives. Serve on 4 warmed plates or bowls.

Photograph page 24

Grain and Buckwheat Noodle Feast

Serves 4
Preparation time: 35 mins
2200 kcal/9240 kJ

---

100 g/*4 oz*/*¹/₂ cup* mixed grains (oats, corn, barley, rye)

1 quantity Egg Pasta Dough (page 10) made with buckwheat flour

1 shallot, finely chopped

100 g/*4 oz*/*¹/₂ cup* butter

1 small carrot, diced

100 g/*4 oz* kohlrabi, diced

salt and pepper

a pinch of grated nutmeg

15 ml/*1 tbsp* water

1 bunch chervil, finely chopped

---

1 Soak the grains overnight in cold water.
2 Roll out the dough very thinly and cut into long strips (noodles). Dust with flour, shaking off any excess.
3 Fry the shallot in half the butter until softened. Add the carrot and kohlrabi to the pan with the drained grains. Cook over a low heat for about 5 minutes.
4 Cook the noodles in plenty of boiling salted water until *al dente*.
5 Season the grains to taste with salt, pepper and nutmeg and add the water. Add the chervil and the remaining butter and stir until the butter melts.

6 Drain the noodles and rinse in hot water. Serve with the mixed grains.

Photograph opposite

Gourmet Tip
It is worth trying to eat with chopsticks as it is not as difficult as you might think. The lower chopstick is held with the thumb over the ring finger. The upper chop stick goes on top of the lower one and is held and moved by the middle finger.
Dried Chinese mushrooms increase quite considerably in volume when they have been soaked in lukewarm water. That is why only a small amount is required for this dish.

Bacon and Onion Pasta Parcels

Serves 4
Preparation time: 50 mins
3200 kcal/13440 kJ

*100 g/**4 oz** finely chopped frozen spinach*
5 small onions
1 clove garlic, crushed
*225 g/**8 oz** minced beef*
1 egg
1 quantity Egg Pasta Dough (page 10)
*100 g/**4 oz** bacon, cut into strips*
*100 g/**4 oz**/¹/₂ cup butter*
salt and pepper
a pinch of grated nutmeg

1 Thaw the spinach and squeeze out the moisture in a cloth. Chop 3 onions finely. Slice 2 thinly.
2 Combine the chopped onions with the garlic, spinach, mince and egg.
3 Divide the dough into 4 and roll out into squares. Fill a piping bag with the meat and pipe 2 sausage shapes on to each pasta square. Moisten the remaining dough and roll it over the mixture.
4 Make small pasta parcels, cutting through the dough between each with a knife and pressing the ends together. Cook in plenty of boiling salted water for 20 minutes.
5 Fry the bacon strips in the butter, then add the onion slices. Season and serve with the pasta.

Photograph (top)

Calves' Liver Ravioli

Serves 4
Preparation time: 50 mins
2700 kcal/11340 kJ

450 g/*1 lb* calves' liver
1 shallot, finely chopped
a little thyme
25 g/*1 oz*/2 tbsp butter
salt and pepper
a pinch of grated nutmeg
3 egg yolks
1 quantity Egg Pasta Dough (page 10)
100 g/*4 oz* fresh spinach, blanched and chopped
200 ml/*7 fl oz*/scant 1 cup double cream
5 ml/*1 tsp* olive or corn oil

1 Dice a quarter of the liver, then fry with shallot and thyme in half the butter. Season. Stir in 1 egg yolk. Leave to cool. **2** Divide dough into 2 and roll out. Place small spoonfuls of liver on one of the pieces at 5cm/2in intervals. Moisten between the liver. Cover with second piece of dough. Press together and cut into rectangular ravioli. **3** Cook in plenty of boiling salted water for 10 minutes. Drain and rinse in hot water. **4** Fry spinach in remaining butter. Stir in 60 ml/4 tbsp cream and season to taste. **5** Whip remaining cream until stiff, then stir in egg yolks. Stir into the spinach and heat through. **6** Brown remaining liver in a pan. Stir oil into the ravioli. Serve with the sauce and liver pieces.
Photograph (bottom)

Creamy Coloured Tagliatelle

Serves 4
Preparation time: 1 hour
3600 kcal/15120 kJ

$^1/_3$ quantity Egg Pasta Dough (page 10)

$^1/_3$ quantity Green Egg Pasta Dough (page 10)

$^1/_3$ quantity Red Egg Pasta Dough (page 11)

30 ml/**2 tbsp** olive or corn oil

250 ml/**8 fl oz**/1 cup double cream

salt and pepper

a pinch of grated nutmeg

2 egg yolks

25 g/**1 oz**/2 tbsp butter

50 g/**2 oz**/$^1/_4$ cup grated Emmethal cheese

---

1 Roll out the doughs very thinly and cut into strips to make tagliatelle.
2 Cook the tagliatelle in plenty of boiling salted water until *al dente*. Drain and rinse in hot water. Toss in the oil.
3 Bring 100 ml/3$^1/_2$ fl oz/6 $^1/_2$ tbsp cream to the boil, then season to taste with salt, pepper and nutmeg.
4 Whip the remaining cream until stiff, then stir in the egg yolks. Mix this thickener into the hot cream and reheat but do not allow to boil.
5 Reheat the tagliatelle in a little water, swirl in the butter and adjust the seasoning if necessary.
6 Serve the tagliatelle and sauce with the cheese over the top.

Photograph front cover

Tagliatelle with Scampi

Serves 4
Preparation time: 45 mins
2200 kcal/9240 kJ

---

350 g/**12 oz** tagliatelle

15 ml/**1 tbsp** olive or corn oil

16 raw scampi

8 small tomatoes, peeled, quartered and seeded

1 shallot, finely chopped

50 g/**2 oz**/$^1/_4$ cup butter

60 ml/**4 tbsp** dry white wine

salt and pepper

1 bunch dill, chopped

a few dill leaves

---

1 Cook the tagliatelle in plenty of boiling salted water until *al dente*. Drain and rinse in hot water. Toss in the oil.
2 Meanwhile, extract the dark vein from the shelled scampi with the point of a knife. Rinse the scampi in cold water.
3 Fry three-quarters of the tomatoes with the shallot in 15 g/$^1/_2$ oz/1 butter until softened. Add the wine.
4 Fry the scampi separately in 15 g/$^1/_2$ oz/1 tbsp butter. As soon as they start to become crispy, turn them over and lower the heat. Cook for a further 2 minutes.
5 Heat up the tagliatelle in a few tablespoons of water and 15 g/$^1/_2$ oz/1 tbsp butter. Season to taste with salt and pepper and arrange on warmed plates.

6 Add the dill and the remaining tomatoes to the sauce, adjust the seasoning if necessary and stir in the remaining butter.
7 Serve the scampi with the tagliatelle and the sauce and garnish with the dill leaves.

Photograph opposite

Gourmet Tip
Tomato segments are easy to prepare. Cut a cross on the top of the tomato and remove the stem. Depending on the size of the tomato, immerse in boiling water for 3 to 10 seconds and transfer immediately to cold water. Slide off the skins, quarter the tomatoes and remove the seeds.

Baked Pasta with Thyme

Serves 4
Preparation time: 60 mins
2500 kcal/10500 kJ

---

350 g/*12 oz* mixed pasta shapes

15 ml/*1 tbsp* olive or corn oil

120 ml/*4 fl oz*/*¹/₂* cup double cream

3 eggs

100 g/*4 oz* boiled ham, cut into strips

100 g/*4 oz* Emmenthal cheese, grated

salt and pepper

5 g/*1 tsp* butter

a little fresh thyme

---

1 Cook the pasta in plenty of boiling salted water until al dente. Drain and rinse in hot water. Toss in the oil.
2 Stir together the cream, eggs, ham and cheese. Season to taste with salt and pepper.
3 Butter a shallow ovenproof dish, spoon in the pasta and pour over the cream and egg mixture.
4 Bake in a pre-heated oven at 180°C/350°F/gas mark 3 for 15 minutes. Sprinkle over the thyme and cook for a further 5 minutes.

Photograph opposite (bottom)

Green Baked Lasagne

Serves 4
Preparation time: 60 mins
2800 kcal/11760 kJ

---

1 quantity Green Pasta Dough (page 10)

450 g/*1 lb* lean minced beef

15 ml/*1 tbsp* olive or corn oil

4 tomatoes, skinned and chopped

1 shallot, finely chopped

1 clove garlic, crushed

45 ml/*3 tbsp* double cream

45 ml/*3 tbsp* tomato purée

150 g/*5 oz* fresh spinach, blanched and finely chopped

salt and pepper

15 g/*¹/₂ oz*/*1 tbsp* butter

100 g/*4 oz* Cheddar or Gruyère cheese, grated

---

1 Roll out the dough thinly and cut several pieces to fit a 20 cm/8 in ovenproof dish. Cook the lasagne sheets for a few minutes in plenty of boiling salted water. Drain and rinse in hot water and lay them on a damp cloth.
2 Fry the beef in the oil. Do not stir, to ensure that none of the juices are extracted. Add the tomatoes, shallot, garlic, cream and tomato purée to the pan. Mix in the spinach and season to taste with salt and pepper.

3 Butter the dish and line it with a sheet of lasagne. Alternate layers of pasta and meat, finishing with a layer of pasta. Sprinkle with the cheese and do with the remaining butter. Bake in a preheated oven at 200°C/400°F/gas mark 6 for 30 minutes.

Photograph opposite (top)

Gourmet Tip
Whenever you blanch vegetables, always rinse them immediately in cold water. Cooking them quickly will enable them to retain their colour and lose less vitamins. The vegetables should not be left in water but kept in a sieve until needed.

Spätzle with Green Lentils

Serves 4
Preparation time: 50 mins
plus soaking
2500 kcal/10500 kJ

100 g/4 oz continental lentils	
225 g/8 oz wholewheat flour, sieved	
4 eggs	
30 ml/2 tbsp olive or corn oil	
40 g/1½ oz/3 tbsp butter	
salt and pepper	
a pinch of grated nutmeg	
50 g/2 oz bacon, diced	
1 small onion, chopped	

1 Soak the lentils overnight in cold water.
2 Mix together the flour, eggs and 15 ml/1 tbsp oil. Knead until dough forms bubbles and is smooth and elastic. Cover and leave to rest in a cool place for 15 minutes.
3 Place a small amount of the dough on a board at a time and cut off thick strips. Cook in boiling salted water until they float to the top. Drain and rinse in cold water. Toss in the remaining oil. Reheat the spätzle in one third of the butter and season with salt, pepper and nutmeg.
4 Cook the bacon and onion in half the remaining butter and 15 ml/1 tbsp water. Stir in the remaining butter and serve.

Photograph opposite (bottom)

Red Ravioli with Walnut Sauce

Serves 4
Preparation time: 50 mins
3500 kcal/14700 kJ

---

100 g/**4 oz** ground walnuts

250 ml/**8 fl oz**/1 cup double cream

75 g/**3 oz** Ricotta cheese

1 egg, separated

pepper

1 quantity Red Pasta Dough (see page 11)

salt

25 g/**1 oz**/2 tbsp butter

2 egg yolks

a few whole walnuts

---

1 Mix the walnuts with 75 ml/5 tbsp cream. Drain the cheese, mix with the egg yolk and season.
2 Halve the dough and roll out thinly. Put half teaspoonfuls of the cheese mixture at 5 cm/2 in intervals on one of the sheets. Dot the surrounding area with whisked egg white. Lay the second piece over the top and press down. Cut out half moon shapes with a pastry cutter.
3 Cook in boiling salted water for 5 minutes. Drain and rinse. Season and swirl in the butter.
4 Heat the walnut and cream mixture. Whip the remaining cream and stir in the egg yolks. Stir into the sauce, bring to the boil and season. Serve garnished with walnuts.

Photograph (top)

Tuna Fettuccine

Serves 4
Preparation time: 45 mins
3800 kcal/15960 kJ

350 g/12 oz fettuccine
75 ml/5 tbsp olive or corn oil
350 g/12 oz tuna fish
1 garlic clove, crushed
1 shallot, finely chopped
5 egg yolks
200 ml/7 fl oz/scant 1 cup double cream
salt and pepper
25 g/1 oz butter
30 ml/2 tbsp capers
1 bunch chives, finely chopped

1 Cook the fettuccine in plenty of boiling salted water until *al dente*. Drain and rinse in hot water. Toss in 15 ml/1 tbsp oil.
2 Keep a little tuna to one side and work the rest to a fine purée with the garlic, shallot, remaining oil, 3 egg yolks and 50 ml/2 fl oz/¼ cup cream. Heat the sauce and season.
3 Whip the remaining cream until stiff, then stir in the remaining 2 egg yolks. Stir into the sauce and bring to the boil.
4 Divide the sauce between warmed plates. Reheat the fettuccine in the butter and place on top. Arrange the tuna chunks on top and sprinkle over the capers and chives.

Photograph opposite (top)

Fettuccine with Mushrooms

Serves 4
Preparation time: 35 mins
2200 kcal/9240 kJ

350 g/12 oz fettuccine
15 ml/1 tbsp olive or corn oil
350 g/12 oz mixed red, green and yellow peppers
1 shallot, finely chopped
100 g/4 oz butter
100 g/4 oz cup mushrooms, cut into quarters or eighths
salt and pepper
a pinch of grated nutmeg

1 Cook the fettuccine in plenty of boiling salted water until *al dente*. Drain and rinse in hot water. Toss in the oil.
2 Wash the peppers, cut into quarters, remove the seeds and cut the flesh into strips. Blanch in boiling water, rinse in cold water and leave to drain.
3 Fry the shallot in most of the butter until softened, then add the peppers and cook for a further minute or so. Add the mushrooms and cook for a further minute.
4 Heat up the pasta with a little water and the remaining butter and season to taste with salt, pepper and nutmeg. Mix in the vegetables and serve on warmed plates.

Photograph opposite (bottom)

Pasta Salads

In the next few pages are pasta salads that are lightly dressed and aimed at the figure-conscious. Even without rich dressings, they are delicious both to the eye and the palate.

Spaghetti and Parma Ham Salad, page 40

39

Spaghetti and Parma Ham Salad

Serves 4
Preparation time: 30 mins
2200 kcal/9240 kJ

---

350 g/12 oz spaghetti

15 ml/1 tbsp olive or corn oil

1 small carrot, cut into matchstick strips

1/2 small kohlrabi, cut into matchstick strips

100 g/4 oz Parma ham, cut into strips

1 bunch tarragon

1 shallot, finely chopped

salt

pepper

white wine vinegar

---

1 Cook the spaghetti in plenty of boiling salted water until al dente. Drain and rinse in cold water. Toss in the oil.
2 Blanch the carrot and kohlrabi strips in lightly salted boiling water for a minute, then rinse immediately in cold water. Leave to drain until required.
3 Reserve a quarter of the ham for decoration, then slice the remainder even finer and place in a bowl.
4 Wash the tarragon and pick off the leaves. Reserve a quarter, then chop the remainder finely.
5 Mix all the salad ingredients together in a bowl and stir in the spaghetti. Season to taste with salt, pepper and wine vinegar.

6 Arrange the salad on plates and garnish with the reserved ham and tarragon leaves.

Photograph page 38

> **Gourmet Tip**
> You can use any kind of ham for this recipe.

Vegetable Twist Salad

Serves 4
Preparation time: 40 mins
1900 kcal/7980 kJ

---

350 g/12 oz pasta spirals

30 ml/2 tbsp olive or corn oil

1/2 yellow pepper, coarsely chopped

1/2 red pepper, coarsely chopped

1/2 green pepper, coarsely chopped

1/2 small courgette, coarsely chopped

1 small carrot, coarsely chopped

1/2 kohlrabi, coarsely chopped

salt

pepper

15 ml/1 tbsp white wine vinegar

1 bunch sorrel or 100 g/4 oz fresh spinach, thoroughly washed

---

1 Cook the pasta spira in plenty of boiling salte water until al dente. Drai and rinse in cold wate Toss in 15 ml/1 tbsp oil.
2 Blanch the vegetable quickly in boiling salte water, then rinse in col water and mix with th pasta.
3 Season to taste with sa and pepper and stir in th remaining oil and th white wine vinegar. C the sorrel or spinach int fine strips and add to th salad.
Variation
You can use whatev vegetables are in seasc for this salad. Different fla voured vinegars, incluc ing balsamic vinegar, ca also be used.

Photograph opposite

Fettuccine and Seafood Salad

Serves 4
Preparation time: 45 mins
1500 kcal/6300 kJ

---

225 g/*8 oz* fettuccine

30 ml/*2 tbsp* olive oil

1 small radiccio (red 'lettuce')

350 g/*12 oz* white fish fillet (cod, plaice, haddock)

450 g mussels, boiled and removed from shells

4 peeled scampi

1 shallot, finely chopped

salt

pepper

15 ml/*1 tbsp* white wine vinegar

---

1 Cook the fettuccine in plenty of boiling salted water until *al dente*. Drain and rinse in cold water. Toss in 15 ml/1 tbsp oil.
2 Wash the radiccio, drain and cut into fine strips.
3 Remove any bones from the fish and cut into bite-sized pieces.
4 Place the fish, mussels and scampi in a saucepan with a little water. Cover the pan and bring to the boil. Remove from the heat as soon as the water has started to boil and leave the fish to cool.
5 Mix together the pasta, radiccio, shallot, mussels and scampi and season to taste with salt and pepper. Add the remaining oil, a little fish stock and the white wine vinegar or lemon juice.

6 Divide the salad between 4 plates and serve the fish on top.

Gourmet Tip
You can make this dish with any kind of fish that you like. Just make sure that it is as fresh as possible and use it the same day.

Chicken and Cucumber Salad

Serves 4
Preparation time: 30 mins
2200 kcal/9240 kJ

225 g/*8 oz* tagliatelle

30 ml/*2 tbsp* olive or corn oil

1 small cucumber

1 bunch dill

3 tomatoes

350 g/*12 oz* chicken breast

15 ml/*1 tbsp* olive or grapeseed oil

15 ml/*1 tbsp* white wine or raspberry vinegar

salt

pepper

1 Cook the tagliatelle in plenty of boiling salted water until *al dente*. Drain and rinse in cold water. Toss in 15 ml/1 tbsp oil.
2 Slice one-third of the cucumber finely. Cut the rest into quarters, remove the seeds and slice finely.
3 Wash the dill and reserve a few sprigs for decoration. Chop the rest up finely.
4 Cut out the stems from the tomatoes and blanch in boiling salted water for a few seconds. Rinse in cold water, skin and chop into bite-sized pieces.
5 Remove the skin from the chicken breasts and cut the flesh into chunks. Arrange the whole cucumber slices on 4 plates.
6 Mix together the pasta, remaining cucumber, dill and tomatoes with the olive or grapeseed oil, vinegar, salt and pepper and lay the mixture on top of the cucumber slices.
7 Season the chicken breasts with salt and pepper and fry in the remaining oil until crispy on the outside and cooked through.
8 Arrange the chicken on top of the salad and garnish with dill.

Photograph opposite (top)

Spaghetti Salad Vinaigrette with Parmesan

Serves 4
Preparation time: 35 mins
2500 kcal/10500 kJ

225 g/*8 oz* spaghetti

15 ml/*1 tbsp* olive or corn oil

75 g/*3 oz* pistachio nuts, blanched in boiling water

15 ml/*1 tbsp* tarragon vinegar

90 ml/*6 tbsp* nut or olive oil

salt

pepper

100 g/*4 oz* cherry tomatoes cut into quarters

1 small frisée lettuce

150 g/*5 oz* Parmesan cheese, finely sliced

1 Cook the spaghetti in plenty of boiling salted water until *al dente*. Drain and rinse in cold water. Toss in the oil and leave to drain.
2 Peel the pistachios and chop up coarsely.
3 Make a vinaigrette by mixing the tarragon vinegar with the nut or olive oil and seasoning to taste with salt and pepper. Mix the spaghetti, pistachios and tomatoes with the dressing.
4 Arrange the frisée lettuce decoratively on plates with the spaghetti salad and Parmesan cheese on top.

Photograph opposite (bottom)

Brown Pasta Spirals with Emmenthal and Ham

Serves 4
Preparation time: 30 mins
2300 kcal/9660 kJ

---

225 g/8 oz brown pasta spirals

---

30 ml/2 tbsp olive or corn oil

---

100 g/4 oz Parma ham, finely sliced

---

100 g/4 oz Emmenthal cheese, finely sliced

---

1 small onion, finely chopped

---

salt

---

pepper

---

15 ml/1 tbsp white wine vinegar

---

1 Cook the pasta spirals in plenty of boiling salted water until *al dente*. Drain and rinse in cold water. Toss in 15 ml/1 tbsp oil.
2 Place the pasta in a bowl and mix in the ham, cheese and onion. Season to taste with salt and pepper and stir in the remaining oil and the wine vinegar.

Photograph (left)

Herb-Cream Fettuccine

Serves 4
Preparation time: 40 mins
1300 kcal/5460 kJ

225 g/*8 oz* fettuccine

30 ml/*2 tbsp* olive or corn oil

1 bunch mixed herbs

120 ml/*4 fl oz*/^{1}/$_2$ cup creme fraîche

50 ml/*2 fl oz*/^{1}/$_4$ cup double cream

15 ml/*1 **tbsp*** lemon juice

salt

pepper

1 small lollo rosso lettuce or
1 small oak-leaf lettuce

1 Cook the pasta in plenty of boiling salted water until *al dente*. Drain and rinse in cold water. Toss in 15 ml/1 tbsp oil.
2 Chop up two-thirds of the herbs and mix together with the creme fraîche, cream, the remaining oil and the lemon juice. Season to taste with salt and pepper.
3 Mix the remaining herbs with the fettuccine and season to taste with salt and pepper. Arrange the pasta on 4 plates and place a few lettuce leaves on top of each. Spoon some of the dressing over the lettuce leaves.
Variation
The herb-cream dressing goes well with crunchy lettuce. Choose a lettuce with some eye-catching red in it.

Photograph (right)

Pasta Soups

Pasta soup is always a popular dish as it is warming and sustaining. The following chapter introduces some new, interesting alternatives.

Vegetable Soup with Tortellini, page 50

Vegetable Soup with Tortellini

Serves 4
Preparation time: 50 mins
2200 kcal/9240 kJ

100 g/4 oz fresh spinach, blanched and finely chopped

75 g/3 oz Ricotta cheese

1 egg yolk

pepper

¹/₂ quantity Egg Pasta Dough (page 10)

50 g/2 oz mushrooms, cut into eighths

¹/₂ red pepper, deseeded and finely chopped

¹/₂ green pepper, deseeded and finely chopped

¹/₂ small courgette, finely chopped

1 small carrot, finely chopped

1 small onion, finely chopped

1 small leek, finely sliced

1 clove garlic, crushed

25 g/1 oz/2 tbsp butter

salt

1 Mix together the spinach, Ricotta cheese, and egg yolk and season with pepper.
2 Divide the dough in half, roll out thinly and spoon half teaspoonfuls of the Ricotta cheese mixture on to one half of the dough at 5 cm/2 in intervals. Moisten the dough with water and cover with the second half of the dough. Mark out half moon-shaped pasta parcels with a glass, cut out and press the edges together.
3 Cook the tortellini in plenty of boiling salted water for about 5 minutes. Drain and rinse in hot water.
4 Meanwhile, fry the vegetables in the butter until soft. Season to taste with salt and pepper, pour in 750 ml/1¹/₄ pts/3 cups boiling water, bring back to the boil and adjust the seasoning if necessary.
5 Pour the soup into warmed dishes and add some tortellini to each dish.

Photograph page 48

Gourmet Tip
Ricotta cheese is made from sheep's milk. If you are unable to buy this, you could use a goats' milk or similar cows' milk cheese for the tortellini filling.

Tomato Soup with Pasta Doug Topping

Serves 4
Preparation time: 50 m
1500 kcal/6300 kJ

1 onion, finely chopped

2 cloves garlic, crushed

30 ml/2 tbsp olive or corn

1 kg/2¹/₄ lb tomatoes, chopped

30 ml/2 tbsp tomato purée

120 ml/4 fl oz/¹/₂ cup dry white wine

salt

pepper

¹/₂ quantity Red Pasta Dough (page 11)

1 Fry the onion and gar in the oil until softene Add the tomatoes.
2 After a few minutes, m in the tomato purée a wine. Bring to the boil th pass through a siev Season to taste with s and pepper. Allow t soup to cool, then pc into individual ovenpr dishes.
3 Roll out the dough thi and cut to cover ea dish. Moisten the edg of the dough with wa and press around t edge of each dish. Ba in a preheated oven 160°C/325°F/gas mark for about 25 minutes.

Photograph opposite

Chicken Alphabet Soup

Serves 4
Preparation time: 50 mins
2300 kcal/9600 kJ

---

*100 g/**4 oz** alphabet spaghetti*

*400 g/**1 lb** boneless chicken breast*

*30 ml/**2 tbsp** olive or corn oil*

¼ courgette, finely chopped

1 red pepper, finely chopped

1 green pepper, finely chopped

*100 ml/**3½ fl oz**/6½ tbsp Marsala*

salt and pepper

a pinch of grated nutmeg

---

1 Cook the spaghetti in plenty of boiling salted water until *al dente*. Drain and rinse in hot water.
2 Skin the chicken and cut into chunks. Fry the chicken in half of the oil in a saucepan until cooked through, then remove from the pan.
3 Fry the vegetables in the remaining oil in the same pan until softened. Add the Marsala to the pan and pour in 1 l/1¾ pts/4¼ cups boiling water or chicken stock.
4 Bring the soup to the boil and add the spaghetti and fried chicken to the pan. Season to taste with salt, pepper and nutmeg and serve.

Photograph (right)

Spinach Soup with Tomato Tagliatelle

Serves 4
Preparation time: 50 mins
2500 kcal/10500 kJ

¹/₂ quantity Red Pasta Dough (page 11)
15 ml/**1 tbsp** olive or corn oil
350 g/**12 oz** fresh spinach, blanched
300 ml/¹/₂ **pt**/1¹/₄ cups double cream
1 small onion, finely chopped
2 cloves garlic, crushed
15 g/¹/₂ **oz**/1 tbsp butter
salt
pepper
a pinch of grated nutmeg
2 egg yolks

1 Roll out the pasta dough thinly and cut into strips. Cook the tagliatelle in plenty of boiling salted water until *al dente*. Drain and rinse in hot water. Toss in the oil.
2 Purée the spinach, then mix in 175 ml/6 fl oz/³/₄ cup cream.
3 Fry the onion and garlic in the butter until softened. Stir in the spinach mixture and pour in 500 ml/18 fl oz/2¹/₄ cups boiling water. Bring back to the boil and season.
4 Reheat the tagliatelle in the soup. Whip the remaining cream until stiff, then stir in the egg yolks. Stir into the soup, bring it back to the boil and serve.

Photograph (left)

53

Herb and Noodle Soup

Serves 4
Preparation time: 30 mins
1500 kcal/6300 kJ

---

150 g/5 oz fine egg noodles, such as vermicelli

2 bunches mixed herbs

1 shallot, finely chopped

40 g/1¹/₂ oz/3 tbsp butter

1 small clove garlic, crushed

salt

pepper

---

1 Cook the noodles in plenty of boiling salted water until *al dente*. Drain and rinse in hot water.
2 Wash the herbs, pick off the leaves and reserve some for decoration.
3 Fry the shallot gently for 5 minutes in a pan with the butter, garlic and herbs. Pour in about 750 ml/1¹/₄ pts/3 cups boiling water and bring back to the boil.
4 Reheat the noodles in the soup and season to taste with salt and pepper. Serve the soup in warmed dishes and garnish with some of the reserved herbs.

Photograph opposite (top)

Multi-Coloured Fettuccine Fish Soup

Serves 4
Preparation time: 50 mins
2800 kcal/11760 kJ

---

150 g/5 oz coloured fettuccine

15 ml/1 tbsp olive or corn oil

4 scampi

350 g/12 oz fish fillet (halibut, bream, perch, red mullet)

1 shallot, finely chopped

1 clove garlic, crushed

15 g/¹/₂ oz/1 tbsp butter

salt

pepper

a pinch of grated nutmeg

120 ml/4 fl oz/¹/₂ cup dry white wine

450 ml/³/₄pt/2 cups double cream

100 ml/3¹/₂ fl oz/6¹/₂ tbsp crème fraîche

2 egg yolks

---

1 Cook the fettuccine in plenty of boiling salted water until *al dente*. Drain and rinse in hot water. Toss in the oil.
2 Extract the dark vein from the shelled scampi with the point of a knife. Rinse in cold water.
3 Remove any bones from the fish and cut into bite-sized pieces.
4 Fry the shallot and garlic in the butter until softened. Add the fish and scampi to the pan and

season to taste with s
pepper and nutmeg. P
in the wine and bring
the boil.
5 Remove the fish fr
the pan and keep it wa
Add 300 ml/¹/₂ pt/
cups cream and
crème fraîche. Bring
the boil.
6 Whip the remain
cream until stiff, then st
the egg yolks. Stir t
thickener into the soup,
low to bubble up and a
just the seasoning
necessary.
7 Reheat the fettuccine
the soup and serve
warmed dishes with
fish pieces on top.

Photograph opposite (bottom)

Gourmet Tip
If you cannot buy
scampi, any other
small shellfish would
be suitable for this
dish.

Sweet Pasta Dishes

Children and adults alike find sweet pasta dishes hard to resist. A few unusual and sophisticated variations are given in the next few pages.

Sugared Noodles with Lemon Sauce, page 58

Sugared Noodles with Lemon Sauce

Serves 4
Preparation time: 1 hour
3000 kcal/12600 kJ

1 quantity *Sweet Egg Pasta Dough (page 11)*

15 ml/1 tbsp olive or corn oil

100 g/4 oz/½ cup sugar

juice of 3 lemons

3 egg yolks

150 ml/¼ pt/⅔ cup double cream

75 g/3 oz candied fruit

1 Roll out the dough fairly thinly and cut into narrow strips.
2 Cook the noodles in plenty of lightly sugared water until *al dente*. Drain and rinse in hot water. Toss in the oil.
3 Heat half the sugar with the lemon juice and mix the other half with the egg yolks. Whisk the hot lemon juice into the egg yolk mixture and heat gently but do not allow to boil. Pass the sauce through a sieve.
4 Beat the cream until stiff and stir into the sauce. Either leave the sauce to cool, or gently reheat it without boiling. Pour the sauce on to warmed plates.
5 Reheat the noodles with a little water, butter and sugar and add to the lemon sauce. Garnish each plate with thin slices of lemon peel and candied fruit.

Photograph page 56

Fruity Coffee Noodles

Serves 4
Preparation time: 50 mir
2000 kcal/8400 kJ

1 quantity *Sweet Egg Past Dough (page 11) made wi 30 ml/2 tbsp instant coffee powder*

a little sugar

25 g/1 oz hazelnuts

25 g/1 oz walnuts

3 cooking apples

juice of 1 lemon

15 g/½ oz/1 tbsp butter

30 ml/2 tbsp honey

30 ml/2 tbsp double crean

1 Roll out the dough thin and cut into 1 cm/½ strips. Cook in plenty lightly sugared boiling wa ter until *al dente*.
2 Reserve a few nuts f decoration and chop th remainder coarsely.
3 Peel and core the ap ples and cut into sma pieces. Pour over th lemon juice.
4 Heat the butter an honey in a saucepan, ad the apples and finally th nuts and mix well.
5 Drain the noodles an rinse in hot water. Stir the cream.
6 Divide the noodles be tween warmed plates an pour over the apple an nut mixture. Decorate wi the reserved nuts an some coffee powder.

Photograph opposite

59

Fine Noodles with Grated Chocolate

Serves 4
Preparation time: 35 mins
1900 kcal/7980 kJ

1 quantity Sweet Egg Pasta Dough (page 11)
a little sugar
150 ml/¹/₄ pt/²/₃ cup double cream
150 g/5 oz dark chocolate, grated

1 Roll out the dough and cut into thin strips. Cook the noodles very briefly in lightly sugared boiling water until *al dente*. Drain and rinse in hot water. Stir in the cream.
2 Arrange the noodles on warmed plates and sprinkle over the grated chocolate.
Variation
You can use any chocolate you like for this recipe. A chocolate sauce with a dash or orange or chocolate liqueur also goes very well with sweet noodles.

Photograph (left)

Chocolate Ravioli with Vanilla Sauce

Serves 4
Preparation time: 1 hour
2500 kcal/10500 kJ

75 g/3 oz quark or fromage frais
75 g/3 oz/¹/₃ cup sugar
4 egg yolks
300 ml/¹/₂ pt/1 ¹/₄ cups full-cream milk
1 vanilla pod
1 quantity Chocolate Egg Pasta Dough (page 11)
30 ml/2 tbsp double cream

1 Stir together the quark, 15 g/¹/₂ oz/1 tbsp sugar and 1 egg yolk and leave on one side.
2 Bring the milk to the boil with the vanilla pod and simmer for 5 minutes.
3 Meanwhile, beat the remaining egg yolks with the remaining sugar until frothy. Pour on the hot milk and heat, stirring, until thick. Pass through a sieve.
4 Divide the dough in half and roll out thinly. Spoon blobs of the quark mixture on to one of the dough sheets at 5 cm/2 in intervals. Moisten the dough and cover with the second piece. Press together and cut out the ravioli.
5 Cook the ravioli in lightly sugared boiling water for about 10 minutes. Drain and rinse in hot water. Toss in the cream and serve with the sauce.

Photograph (right)

Sugar-Cinnamon Noodles

Serves 4
Preparation time: 40 mins
1800 kcal/7560 kJ

1 quantity Sweet Egg Pasta Dough (page 11)
a little sugar
30 ml/2 tbsp double cream
40 g/1½ oz/3 tbsp sugar
15 ml/1 tbsp cinnamon
2 kiwi fruit, peeled and sliced
1 pear, peeled, cored and sliced

1 Roll out the pasta thinly and cut into fairly narrow strips.
2 Cook the noodles briefly in lightly sugared boiling water until *al dente*. Drain and rinse in hot water. Toss in the cream and arrange on warmed plates.
3 Mix together the sugar and cinnamon and sprinkle over the noodles. Arrange the fruit around the edge.

Photograph opposite (right)

Raisin and Nut Spaghetti with Strawberries

Serves 4
Preparation time: 30 mins
2000 kcal/8400 kJ

40 g/1½ oz/3 tbsp raisins
225 g/8 oz spaghetti
a little sugar
14 ml/2 tbsp olive or corn oil
100 g/4 oz fresh strawberries
15 g/½ oz/2 tbsp butter
14 ml/1 tbsp honey
40 g/1½ oz/3 tbsp flaked almonds, finely chopped
15 ml/1 tbsp double cream

1 Soak the raisins in lukewarm water for about 30 minutes. Drain.
2 Cook the spaghetti in plenty of lightly sugared boiling water until *al dente*. Drain and rinse in hot water. Drain thoroughly then mix with the oil.
3 Reserve a few strawberries for decoration, then halve or quarter the rest, depending on their size.
4 Heat the butter and honey in a saucepan and stir in the raisins and almonds.
5 Reheat the spaghetti with the cream and arrange on warmed plates. Divide the raisin and almond mixture between the plates and arrange the strawberries on top.

Photograph opposite (left)

Index of Recipes

Foulsham
Yeovil Road, Slough, Berkshire, SL1 4J
ISBN 0-572-01662-X
This English language edition copyrigh
© 1991 W. Foulsham & Co. Ltd.
Originally published by Falken-Verlag,
GmbH, Niedernhausen TS, West
Germany.
Photographs copyright © Falken Verla

Printed in Portugal.